# CELEBRATING THE FAMILY NAME OF CONTRERAS

# Celebrating the Family Name of Contreras

Walter the Educator

**SKB**
Silent King Books
a WhichHead Entertainment Imprint

Copyright © 2024 by Walter the Educator

All rights reserved. No part of this book may be reproduced in any manner whatsoever without written permission except in the case of brief quotations embodied in critical articles and reviews.

First Printing, 2024

Disclaimer

This book is a literary work; the story is not about specific persons, locations, situations, and/or circumstances unless mentioned in a historical context. Any resemblance to real persons, locations, situations, and/or circumstances is coincidental. This book is for entertainment and informational purposes only. The author and publisher offer this information without warranties expressed or implied. No matter the grounds, neither the author nor the publisher will be accountable for any losses, injuries, or other damages caused by the reader's use of this book. The use of this book acknowledges an understanding and acceptance of this disclaimer.

Celebrating the Family Name of Contreras is a memory book that belongs to the Celebrating Family Name Book Series by Walter the Educator. Collect them all and more books at WaltertheEducator.com

**USE THE EXTRA SPACE TO DOCUMENT YOUR FAMILY MEMORIES THROUGHOUT THE YEARS**

# CONTRERAS

In the heart of history's timeless thread,

Lies the name Contreras, vibrant and spread.

A lineage bold, with roots that run deep,

Through mountain and valley, in memories they keep.

Born of a spirit unyielding, profound,

Where courage and honor eternally sound.

The Contreras name, a beacon of pride,

In trials and triumphs, they always reside.

Each letter a symbol, each syllable strong,

A melody woven in ancestral song.

With hands that built dreams, with voices that soar,

The Contreras thrive on life's boundless shore.

From dawn's golden light to twilight's embrace,

Their footsteps carve paths, no time can erase.

They harvest ambition, sowing it wide,

A family united, side by side.

Their laughter like rivers, flowing with ease,

Whispering tales to the swaying trees.

In the warmth of their hearth, a love so true,

An eternal flame, always renewed.

From artisans crafting to scholars who teach,

The Contreras name extends its reach.

Through fields of endeavor, their stories unfold,

Like the glow of the sun in hues of gold.

Bound by their values, resilient they stand,

Fingers entwined, a resolute band.

Their hearts beat as one, in rhythm divine,

Each moment they cherish, each spark they enshrine.

The Contreras endure, like a steadfast star,

Guiding their kin, no matter how far.

Through winds of change and torrents that test,

Their unity proves they are truly blessed.

Oh Contreras, a name so grand and bright,

You carry the past into future's light.

With every new chapter, your essence will grow,

A legacy timeless, forever aglow.

So raise up the banner, proclaim it with cheer,

The name Contreras is treasured and dear.

An emblem of strength, of love without end,

A heritage rich that no force can bend.

# ABOUT THE CREATOR

Walter the Educator is one of the pseudonyms for Walter Anderson. Formally educated in Chemistry, Business, and Education, he is an educator, an author, a diverse entrepreneur, and he is the son of a disabled war veteran. "Walter the Educator" shares his time between educating and creating. He holds interests and owns several creative projects that entertain, enlighten, enhance, and educate, hoping to inspire and motivate you. Follow, find new works, and stay up to date with Walter the Educator™ at WaltertheEducator.com